Delicious Fryer Recipes

A Mouth Watering Selection of Foods

All in One Cookbook

BY

Daniel Humphreys

License Notes

No part of this Book can be reproduced in any form or by any means including print, electronic, scanning or photocopying unless prior permission is granted by the author.

All ideas, suggestions and guidelines mentioned here are written for informative purposes. While the author has taken every possible step to ensure accuracy, all readers are advised to follow information at their own risk. The author cannot be held responsible for personal and/or commercial damages in case of misinterpreting and misunderstanding any part of this Book

Table of Contents

Introduction

You can't deny the fact that there is something extra special about deep fried foods! No matter what you are frying each meal has something individually unique about it that brings a warm and comforting atmosphere to the home. You simply can't resist deep fried foods!

The majority of people are not aware that it doesn't take much effort to make a great deep fried meal. There are no special ingredients, there is no magical way of lowering the food into the fryer, it's really is that simple.

There is so much you can combine with deep fried foods to make an even more spectacular meal. If you are not familiar with what they are, here is a list:

- Mashed potatoes
- Macaroni and cheese
- Collard greens
- Corn bread
- Fried green tomatoes
- Butterbeans
- Fried pecan okra
- Crispy bacon with green peas
- Summer squash casserole
- Fresh corn cakes
- Feta stuffed tomatoes
- Fried confetti corn

There are so many different side dishes you could make I will need to write another cookbook to do them any justice. However, you can work with these for now and I am certain you have your own ideas you can add to the list.

I don't want to spend too much time on this introduction; I'm just as excited as you are to get started! Here are 30 great deep fried mouth-watering recipes for you to enjoy!

1: Deep Fried Breaded Mushrooms

Soft white mushrooms coated in Italian seasoned breadcrumbs.

Preparation time: 9 minutes

Serves: 4 servings

Ingredients

- 8-10 ounces of whole white mushrooms
- ¾ cup of flour
- 2 slightly beaten eggs
- 1 cup of Italian seasoned breadcrumbs
- 1 cup of vegetable oil

Directions

1. Heat the oil in a deep fryer to 375 degrees.

2. Wash the mushrooms and cut off the stems.

3. Dry the mushrooms using a paper towel.

4. Pour the flour into a small bowl and coat the mushrooms lightly.

5. Slightly beat the eggs in another small bowl and dip the mushrooms in the eggs.

6. Pour the breadcrumbs into another small bowl and coat the mushrooms.

7. Set the batter by leaving the mushrooms on a rack for 2 minutes.

8. Deep fry the mushrooms in batches until they turn golden brown in color, this should take approximately 4 minutes.

9. Drain the mushrooms on paper towels and serve.

2: Deep Fried Coca Cola

Sounds strange but tastes delicious!

Preparation time: 40 minutes

Serves: 6 servings

Ingredients

- 3 large eggs
- 2 cups of coca-cola
- ¼ cup of granulated sugar
- 3 ½ cups of all purpose flour
- 2 teaspoons of baking powder
- ½ a teaspoon of salt
- Vegetable oil
- Powdered sugar
- Pure cola syrup

Ingredients for garnish (optional)

- Maraschino cherries
- Whipped cream

Directions

1. Heat the oil in a deep fryer to 375 degrees.

2. Beat the eggs in a large bowl and then add the granulated sugar and the coca cola.

3. Sift the salt, baking powder and 2 cups of flour into the coke mixture. Stir while adding and ensure that the batter is not too thick and smooth.

4. Spoon 1 ½ inch dough balls into the deep fryer and cook until they become golden brown. This should take approximately 3 minutes.

5. Use a slotted spoon to remove them from the deep fryer and place them on paper towels to drain the oil.

6. Sprinkle powdered sugar over the coke balls and cola syrup while they are still hot.

7. If desired garnish with maraschino cherries and whipped cream.

3: Mouth Watering Apple Fritters

If you have a sweet tooth, this recipe will definitely satisfy it!

Preparation time: 35 minutes

Serves: 30 servings

Ingredients

- Vegetable oil
- All purpose flour, 2 cups
- ½ a cup of granulated sugar
- 3 tablespoons of granulated sugar
- 2 ¼ teaspoons of baking powder
- 2 teaspoons of ground cinnamon
- 1 ¼ teaspoons of salt
- A pinch of salt
- 2 large eggs
- ¾ cup of whole milk
- 2 tablespoons of melted butter
- 2 teaspoons of pure vanilla
- 2 apples, cut into pieces and cored
- Powdered sugar (optional)

Directions

1. Heat the oil in a deep fryer to 375 degrees.

2. In a large bowl add the flour, ground cinnamon, baking powder, sugar and a pinch of salt.

3. Crack the eggs into another large bowl and whisk them thoroughly.

4. Add the pure vanilla, melted butter, the whole milk and whisk to combine.

5. Add the mixture to the dry Ingredients and stir to combine.

6. Add the apples and stir to combine.

7. Drop spoonfuls of batter into the deep fryer and fry until golden brown, this should take approximately 6-8 minutes.

8. Line a plate with paper towels and drain the apple fritters.

9. If desired, dust the fritters with the powdered sugar and serve while hot.

4: Deep Fried Classic Chicken

This is a tasty authentic fried chicken recipe that you can serve with green beans and mashed potatoes for the tastiest results!

Preparation time: 3 hours

Serves: 4-6 servings

Ingredients

- One 8 ounce chicken cut into pieces
- 1 tablespoon of salt
- 2 teaspoons of black pepper
- 1 teaspoon of powdered garlic
- ½ a cup of hot sauce
- ½ a cup of buttermilk
- 3 large eggs
- Peanut oil
- 2 ½ cups of self raising flour

Directions

1. Heat the oil in a deep fryer to 375 degrees C.

2. Preheat the oven to 200 degrees C.

3. Season the chicken with the garlic powder, black pepper and a pinch of salt.

4. In a large bowl combine the eggs, buttermilk and hot sauce. Add the chicken pieces and coat them well with the mixture.

5. Put a cover over the bowl and marinate it in the fridge for 2 hours.

6. Pour the all purpose flour into a bowl, remove the chicken from the fridge and dunk the chicken in the flour.

7. Fry for 10 minutes in the deep fryer.

8. Transfer the chicken onto a baking sheet and bake in the oven for 10 minutes.

9. Once cooked, serve immediately.

5: Tasty Deep Fried Turkey

If you want to impress your friends and family members on Thanksgiving Day, this is definitely the recipe to do so!

Preparation time: 2 hours 45 minutes

Serves: 8 servings

Ingredients

- One 12 pound turkey
- Salt
- Black pepper
- Vegetable oil

Directions

1. Heat the oil in a deep fryer until it reaches 375 degrees.

2. Wash the turkey and dry pat it using paper towels.

3. Season inside and outside the turkey with salt and pepper.

4. Place the turkey in the fryer for 45 minutes.

5. Remove the turkey from the deep fryer and let it rest for 30 minutes.

6. Carve and serve it with a side dish of your choice.

6: Deep Fried Onions

There is nothing better than simple but delicious fried onions!

Preparation time: 1 hour 10 minutes

Serves: 4 servings

Ingredients

- 2 tablespoons of mayonnaise
- 2 tablespoons of sour cream
- 1 ½ teaspoons of ketchup
- ½ a teaspoon of Worcestershire sauce
- 1 tablespoon of drained horseradish
- ¼ teaspoon of smoked paprika
- A pinch of cayenne pepper
- Salt
- Black pepper
- Onion Ingredients
- 1 Vidalia onion
- 2 ½ cups of all purpose flour
- 1 teaspoon of cayenne pepper
- 2 tablespoons of smoked paprika
- ½ a teaspoon of dried thyme
- ½ a teaspoon of dried oregano
- ½ a teaspoon of cumin
- Salt
- Black pepper
- 2 large eggs
- 1 cup of whole milk
- 1 gallon of corn oil

Directions

1. Heat the oil in a deep fryer until it reaches 375 degrees.

2. Prepare the dip by combining all the Ingredients in a medium bowl and whisk together thoroughly. Place a lid over the bowl and leave it in the fridge to chill.

3. Slice the onion into rings and put them to one side.

4. In a large bowl combine the ground cumin, dried oregano, dried thyme, smoked paprika, all-purpose flour, cayenne pepper and a pinch of black pepper. Stir to combine the Ingredients.

5. In a small bowl combine one cup of water, the eggs and the whole milk. Whisk the Ingredients together thoroughly.

6. Put the onions in the bowl with the flour mixture. Coat the onions by putting a lid over the bowl and shaking it.

7. Remove the onions from the bowl and place them onto a plate.

8. Dip the onions into the egg mixture and then into the flour again and then into the egg again.

9. Put the onions into a deep fryer and fry until they become golden brown in color. This should take approximately 12 minutes.

10. Arrange paper towels on a plate.

11. Remove the onions from the deep fryer using a slotted spoon and put them onto the plate to drain.

12. Season the onions with a pinch of salt and serve with the dip.

7: Southern Fried Catfish

There is more than one way to make catfish!

Preparation time: 1 hour 10 minutes

Serves: 8 servings

Tartar sauce Ingredients

- 3 tablespoons of extra virgin olive oil
- ¾ cup of mayonnaise
- 2 thinly sliced scallions
- 2 teaspoons of drained sweet pickle relish

Catfish Ingredients

- 1 liter of canola oil
- 3 cups of cornmeal
- 2 tablespoons of Cajun blackfish spice
- Salt
- Pepper
- 4 pounds of catfish fillets
- Fresh lemon wedges to serve

Directions

1. Heat the oil in a deep fryer until it reaches 375 degrees C.

2. In a small bowl combine the drained relish, scallions, mayonnaise and extra virgin olive oil. Whisk together thoroughly and then leave it in the fridge until it is ready to use.

3. In a large bowl combine the Cajun black fish spice, the cornmeal, and the salt and pepper. Stir to combine and then dip the catfish fillets into the mixture.

4. Transfer the fillets into the deep fryer and fry for 10 minutes.

5. Line a plate with paper towels.

6. Remove the catfish from the deep fryer using a slotted spoon and place onto the plate to drain.

7. Serve with the lemon wedges and the tartar sauce.

8: Deep Fried Pork Chops

Tasty pork chops coated in hot sauce, buttermilk and cayenne pepper.

Preparation time: 46 minutes

Serves: 6 servings

Ingredients

- 6 pork chops with the bone
- Salt
- Pepper
- Butter crackers, 2 sleeves
- ¾ cup of all-purpose flour
- ¼ teaspoon of cayenne pepper
- 1 cup of buttermilk
- 1 teaspoon of hot sauce
- Vegetable oil

Directions

1. Lay the pork chops on a chopping board and then beat them using a mallet until they are half an inch thick.

2. Season the pork chops on both sides with salt and pepper.

3. Place the crackers into a zip lock bag and then crush them completely.

4. In a small baking dish combine the cayenne pepper and the all-purpose flour.

5. In another baking dish add the hot sauce and the buttermilk and stir to combine.

6. In another baking dish add the crushed crackers.

7. Coat the pork chops in the flour mixture.

8. Dip the pork chops into the butter mixture.

9. Roll the pork chops into the crackers.

10. Arrange the pork chops onto a baking tray and let them rest for 10 minutes.

11. Put the pork chops into the deep fryer and fry until they become golden brown in color. This should take approximately 16 minutes.

12. Line a plate with paper towels.

13. Remove the pork chops from the deep fryer and drain on the plate.

14. Serve with a side dish of your choice.

9: Sweet Potato Fries

We all know that regular French fries are good, but did you know sweet potato fries tasted even better?

Preparation time: 23 minutes

Serves: 4 servings

Ingredients

- 6 cups of peanut oil
- 1 teaspoon of salt
- ½ a teaspoon of powdered garlic
- ½ a teaspoon of smoked paprika
- 1/8 teaspoon of sugar

- 1 cup of cornstarch
- ¾ cup of club soda
- 2 pounds of sweet potatoes sliced into ½ inch thick pieces

Directions

1. Heat the peanut oil in a deep fryer until it reaches 375 degrees C.

2. In a large bowl combine the sugar, smoked paprika, powdered garlic and salt. Stir to combine and set to one side.

3. In another large bowl add the club soda and the cornstarch.

4. Dip the sweet potato fries into the smoked paprika mixture and then into the cornstarch mixture.

5. Place them into the deep fryer and cook until they become golden brown, this should take approximately 8 minutes.

6. Line a plate with paper towels.

7. Remove the sweet potatoes fries from the deep fryer and drain them on the plate.

8. Season the fries with the garlic powder and serve.

10: Deep Fried Ravioli

Delicious deep fried ravioli coated in Italian breadcrumbs and Romano cheese.

Preparation time: 19 minutes

Serves: 6 to 8 servings

Ingredients

- Vegetable oil
- 3 large eggs
- All-purpose flour
- 2 cups of Italian breadcrumbs
- One 9 ounce packet of ravioli
- Grated Romano cheese
- Fresh parsley, chopped
- Marinara sauce

Directions

1. Heat the oil in a deep fryer until it reaches 375 degrees C.

2. Crack the eggs into a small bowl and whisk them.

3. In another small bowl add the flour.

4. In another small bowl add the breadcrumbs and season them with salt and pepper.

5. Dip the ravioli into the eggs.

6. Coat the ravioli with the flour.

7. Dip the ravioli back into the eggs.

8. Coat the ravioli with the breadcrumbs.

9. Repeat the process with all pieces of ravioli.

10. Place the ravioli into the deep fryer and fry until golden brown; this should take approximately 4 minutes.

11. Line a plate with paper towels.

12. Remove the ravioli from the deep fryer and drain them on the plate.

13. Top the ravioli with the grated cheese and the fresh parsley and serve with the marinara sauce.

11: Deep Fried Corn Muffin Churros

Delicious fried churros dipped in chocolate sauce.

Preparation time: 1 hour 30 minutes

Serves: 24 servings

Ingredients

- Vegetable oil
- One box of corn muffin mix
- All-purpose flour, 1 ½ cups
- 1/3 cup of sugar
- Sugar for sprinkling
- 1 teaspoon of baking powder
- 2 teaspoons of ground cinnamon
- 2 large eggs
- 1 teaspoon of grated orange zest
- 2/3 cup of buttermilk
- Chocolate sauce

Directions

1. Heat the oil in a deep fryer until it reaches 375 degrees C.

2. In a large bowl combine 1 teaspoon of cinnamon, baking powder, all-purpose flour and the corn muffin mix, stir to combine.

3. Add the buttermilk, orange zest and eggs, and stir to combine.

4. Fit a star tip onto a large pastry bag and pour the batter into it. Pipe strips 4 inches in length into the deep fry and fry on both sides until they become golden brown in color, this should take approximately 1 minute.

5. Line a plate with paper towels.

6. Remove the churros from the deep fryer and drain on the plate.

7. In a small bowl combine the sugar and remaining cinnamon, stir to combine and sprinkle onto the churros.

8. Serve with the chocolate sauce.

12: Salmon Croquettes Breakfast

Fried fish for breakfast! Can it get any better?

Preparation time: 35 minutes

Serves: 15 servings

Ingredients

- 8 ounces of baked and flaked salmon
- 2 large eggs, beaten
- 2 cups of mashed potatoes
- 1 diced white onion
- 5 cloves of minced garlic

- Salt
- Black pepper
- 6 tablespoons of all purpose flour
- Peanut oil

Directions

1. In a large bowl combine the onions, salmon, garlic, mashed potatoes and eggs. Season with salt and pepper and stir to combine.

2. Using your hands, mould the mixture in to small circles, the size of golf balls. Put them into a bowl, cover and allow them to chill in the fridge overnight.

3. Heat the oil in a deep fryer until it reaches 375 degrees C.

4. Add the croquettes and fry until they turn golden brown in color, this should take approximately 5 minutes.

5. Line a plate with paper towels.

6. Remove the croquettes from the deep fryer, let them drain on the plate and serve.

13: Deep Fried Doughnuts

Mouth-watering deep fried doughnuts topped with confetti sprinkles.

Preparation time: 1 hour

Serves: 12 servings

Doughnut Ingredients

- Cooking spray
- 3 cups of all-purpose flour
- 3 tablespoons of confetti sprinkles
- 1 tablespoon of baking powder
- Salt
- ¾ cup of sugar
- 3 tablespoons of unsalted butter
- 2 large eggs
- 1 tablespoon of pure vanilla
- ½ a cup of whole milk
- Vegetable oil

Chocolate frosting Ingredients

- 1/2 a cup of powdered cocoa
- 4 tablespoons of melted unsalted butter
- 1 ½ teaspoons of pure vanilla
- 3 cups of confectioner's sugar
- ¼ cup of whole milk

Directions

1. Heat the oil in a deep fryer until it reaches 375 degrees C.

2. On a sheet of paper draw 12 three inch circles. Turn the paper over and place it onto a large baking sheet. Spray the sheet with the cooking spray and put it to one side.

3. Fit a ½ inch long pastry tip onto a pastry bag and set it to one side.

4. In a medium sized bowl combine the baking powder, a pinch of salt, the sprinkles and the all-purpose flour. Stir to combine.

5. In a large bowl combine the butter and the sugar and blend with a handheld electric blender until it turns into a creamy consistency. This should take approximately 2 minutes. Add the pure vanilla and the eggs and continue to whisk until the mixture turns into a pale color.

6. Pour the batter into the pastry bag.

7. Pipe the batter onto the parchment paper and leave it in the refrigerator to chill for 30 minutes.

8. Fry the doughnuts in batches for 2 minutes on each side.

9. Line a plate with paper towels.

10. Remove the doughnuts from the deep fryer and drain on the plate.

11. In a small bowl combine the pure vanilla, melted butter, powdered cocoa and a pinch of salt. Use a hand held mixer to combine.

12. Add the whole milk and the confectioners' sugar and continue to mix until the Ingredients turn into a smooth consistency.

13. When the doughnuts cool down spread the chocolate frosting over them and then sprinkle the confetti over the top and serve.

14: Deep Fried Beignets

Scrumptious fried beignets coated with powdered sugar.

Preparation time: 3 hours 40 minutes

Serves: 24 servings

Ingredients

- 1 teaspoon of active dry yeast
- ¾ cups of warm water
- ¼ cup of granulated sugar
- ½ a teaspoon of salt
- 1 large egg
- ½ a cup of evaporated milk
- All-purpose flour, 3 ½ cups
- 1/8 a cup of vegetable shortening
- Peanut oil, 8 cups
- Powdered sugar

Directions

1. In a large bowl combine the warm water and yeast and let it sit for 5 minutes until it turns into a foam.

2. Add the milk, egg, a pinch of salt and the granulated sugar and whisk with a handheld mixer.

3. Add the all-purpose flour and continue to whisk until the Ingredients become smooth.

4. Add the vegetable shortening and continue to whisk until completely combined.

5. Cover the bowl and leave it in the fridge for 3 hours.

6. Heat the oil in a deep fryer until it reaches 375 degrees C.

7. Take the mixture out of the fridge and use a rolling pin to roll out 1/8 an inch of dough.

8. Slice the dough into ½ inch length squares.

9. Fry the squares on both sides until they become light brown in color, this should take approximately 3 minutes.

10. Line a plate with paper towels.

11. Remove the squares from the deep fryer and allow them to drain.

12. Sprinkle the squares with the powdered sugar and serve.

15: Deep Fried Mozzarella Planks

Yummy, stingy, fried cheese!

Preparation time: 1 hour and 10 minutes

Serves: 4 servings

Ingredients

- 8 ¼ inch thick mozzarella and cheese planks
- 1 cup of whole milk
- 1 large egg, beaten
- All-purpose flour, 2 cups
- 1 tablespoon of salt
- 1 teaspoon of white pepper
- 3 cups of breadcrumbs
- 2 tablespoons of fresh minced parsley
- 1 teaspoon of powdered garlic
- Vegetable oil
- Tangy marinara sauce

Directions

1. Freeze the planks of cheese for 20 minutes.

2. In a large bowl combine the parmesan cheese, all purpose flour, a pinch of salt and black pepper. Stir to combine.

3. In a medium bowl, combine the powdered garlic, the minced parsley and the bread crumbs. Stir to combine.

4. In a small bowl crack the egg and whisk it.

5. Remove the cheese planks from the freezer and dip them into the flour mixture.

6. Brush both sides of the cheese planks with the egg.

7. Roll the cheese planks into the breadcrumbs and then lay them onto a baking sheet.

8. Put the cheese planks back into the freezer for 30 minutes.

9. Heat the oil in a deep fryer until it reaches 375 degrees C.

10. Remove the cheese planks from the freezer and fry until they become golden brown in color, this should take approximately 10 minutes.

11. Line a plate with paper towels.

12. Remove the cheese planks from the deep fryer and drain on the plate.

13. Serve with the marinara sauce.

16: Deep Fried Buffalo Chicken Wings

Adorable buffalo chicken wings with blue cheese dip.

Preparation time: 1 hour and 20 minutes

Serves: 4 servings

Ingredients

- Vegetable oil
- 3 pounds of chicken wings
- 5 sticks of celery sliced into dip sized pieces
- ¼ cup of hot sauce
- 1 tablespoon of fresh lemon juice

Blue cheese dip Ingredients

- 6 ounces of crumbled blue cheese
- Sour cream, 1 cup
- A pinch of salt
- Mayonnaise, ¾ cup
- 1 tablespoon of fresh lemon juice
- Salt
- Pepper
- Hot sauce
- 1 teaspoon of powdered garlic

Directions

1. Heat the oil in a deep fryer until it reaches 375 degrees C.

2. Wash and pat dry the chicken wings.

3. Place the chicken into the deep fryer and fry until crispy, this should take approximately 7 minutes.

4. Line a plate with paper towels.

5. Remove the chicken from the deep fryer and drain them on the plate.

6. Heat a small saucepan on medium heat and melt the butter.

7. Add the hot sauce, lemon juice and some salt and pepper to the butter.

8. Whisk the hot sauce mixture together and pour it into a large bowl.

9. Transfer the chicken wings into the large bowl and coat them with the sauce.

10. In a medium sized bowl combine the Ingredients and whisk together thoroughly. Place a lid over the bowl and set it to one side.

11. Crumble the top of the sauce and serve with the chicken wings and celery sticks.

17: Hush Puppie Crab with Jalapeno Dip

Delightful fried crab with jalapeno dip.

Preparation time: 30 minutes

Serves: 18 servings

Hush puppie Ingredients

- Cornmeal, 1 ½ cups
- ½ a cup of all purpose flour
- 2 teaspoons of baking powder
- 2 teaspoons of salt
- 2 teaspoons of sugar
- 1 teaspoon of powdered garlic
- 1 ½ cups of butter
- 1 large egg
- 8 ounces of jumbo crab meat
- 3 thinly sliced scallions
- Canola oil
- Sea salt

Jalapeno dip Ingredients

- 1 cup of fresh cilantro leaves
- ½ a cup of mayonnaise
- ½ a teaspoon of powdered garlic
- ½ a teaspoon of sea salt
- ¼ teaspoon of black pepper
- The green part of 3 scallions finely chopped
- ½ a jalapeño chopped and seeded

Directions

1. Heat the oil in a deep fryer until it reaches 375 degrees C.

2. In a medium bowl combine the powdered garlic, sugar, a pinch of salt, a pinch of salt, baking powder, all-purpose flour and cornmeal. Stir to combine.

3. In a small bowl combine the egg and buttermilk and whisk together thoroughly.

4. Create a hole in the middle of the dry **Ingredients** and pour the buttermilk mix into it. Stir to combine.

5. Add the sliced scallions and the crab and stir to combine.

6. Make the jalapeño dip by adding the chopped scallions, jalapeno, black pepper, a pinch of salt, powdered garlic, mayonnaise, and cilantro leaves. Blend until the Ingredients become smooth, pour into a small bowl, cover and leave in the fridge until you are ready to use it.

7. Use an ice cream scoop to drop the batter into the deep fryer and fry until golden brown in color; this should take approximately 4 minutes.

8. Line a plate with paper towels.

9. Remove the crab mix from the deep fryer and drain on the plate.

10. Season with salt and serve with the jalapeno dip.

18: Deep Fried Cheese Curd

Enticing deep fried cheese curd with marinara sauce

Preparation time: 30 minutes

Serves: 4 servings

Ingredients

- 1 cup of flour
- 1 ½ teaspoons of baking powder

- ½ a teaspoon of salt
- 1 cup of club soda
- 1 pound of cheese curds
- 4 cups of vegetable oil
- Marinara sauce

Directions

1. Heat the oil in a deep fryer until it reaches 375 degrees C.

2. Combine the club soda, baking powder, flour and salt in a smooth bowl and whisk together thoroughly until smooth.

3. Place the cheese curds into the batter and coat.

4. Fry the cheese curds in batches until they become golden brown in color this should take approximately 5 minutes.

5. Line a plate with paper towels.

6. Remove the cheese curds from the deep fryer and drain on the plate.

7. Serve the cheese curds with the marinara sauce.

19: Deep Fried Balls of Rice

Enjoy a different kind of fried rice.

Preparation time: 1 hour

Serves: 8 servings

Ingredients

- 2 eggs
- 5 tablespoons of grated Parmesan cheese
- 1 tablespoon of dried parsley
- ¼ teaspoon of ground black pepper
- 1 teaspoon of salt
- 1 liter of water
- 185 grams of uncooked white rice
- 160 grams of dried breadcrumbs
- 475ml of olive oil

Directions

1. In a large bowl combine 1 teaspoon of salt, pepper, parsley, cheese and eggs. Whisk together thoroughly place a lid over it and leave it in the fridge.

2. Pour the water into a saucepan and add 1 teaspoon of salt. Bring it to a boil on a high temperature.

3. Reduce the heat to a low temperature and add the rice. Cook until most of the water is absorbed.

4. Take the rice off the heat and add the egg mixture at the same time as stirring quickly to stop the eggs from scrambling.

5. Leave the rice mixture to cool for one hour.

6. Pour the breadcrumbs into a small bowl.

7. Use your hands to mold the rice into small circles the size of ping pong balls.

8. Coat the rice balls with the bread crumbs.

9. Fry the balls in batches until they become golden brown in color. This should take approximately 10 minutes.

10. Line a plate with paper towels.

11. Remove the rice balls from the deep fryer, drain on the plate and serve.

20: Glazed Apple Cider Doughnuts

Heavenly glazed apple cider doughnuts

Preparation time: 1 hour

Serves: 24 servings

Ingredients

- Two 25 ounce envelopes of active dry yeast
- ¼ cup of warm water
- ½ a cup of sugar
- 1/3 cup of shortening
- 1 ½ cups of lukewarm milk
- 2 eggs
- 1 ½ teaspoons of salt
- 1 teaspoon of apple pie spice
- 6 cups of all-purpose flour

Glaze Ingredients

- 4 cups of apple cider
- 5 cups of confectioners' sugar
- ¼ cup of corn syrup
- 4 teaspoons of apple pie spice

Directions

1. Sprinkle the yeast into the water and let it sit for 5 minutes until it starts to foam.

2. In a large bowl combine 2 cups of flour, eggs, apple pie spice, salt, milk, shortening, cream sugar and yeast mixture. Use a handheld electric mixer to combine.

3. Add the rest of the flour ½ a cup at a time and continue to whisk with the hand held mixer.

4. Remove the dough from the bowl and knead it with your hands for approximately 5 minutes.

5. Grease a large bowl and put the kneaded dough into it and place plastic wrap over the top. Leave the dough in a warm place and allow it to rise until it is double the size.

6. Sprinkle flour over a chopping board and roll the dough out until it is half an inch thick.

7. Cover a doughnut cutter with flour and slice the dough.

8. Loosely cover the doughnuts with a cloth and allow them to rise until they are double the size. This should take approximately 2 hours.

9. While the doughnuts are rising make the glaze.

10. Pour the apple cider vinegar into a medium saucepan. Boil on a low temperature until it reduces to 2/3 of a cup.

11. Transfer the apple cider vinegar from the saucepan into a large bowl.

12. Add the apple pie spice, corn syrup and confectioners' sugar and whisk together thoroughly until smooth.

13. Fry the doughnuts two at a time for one minute on each side.

14. Line a plate with paper towels.

15. Remove the doughnuts from the deep fryer and drain on the plate.

16. Dip the doughnuts into the glaze and leave them to dry on a baking rack.

17. Serve the doughnuts when dry, this should take approximately 2 minutes.

21: Deep Fried Shrimp, Japanese-Style

Luscious fried shrimp with a Japanese twist.

Preparation time: 20 minutes

Serves: 4 servings

Ingredients

- 1 pound of medium shrimp, leave the tails on, deveined and peeled
- ½ a teaspoon of salt
- ½ a teaspoon of ground black pepper
- ½ a teaspoon of garlic powder

- 1 teaspoon of paprika
- 1 cup of panko crumbs
- Vegetable oil

Directions

1. Heat the oil in a deep fryer until it reaches 375 degrees C.

2. Season the shrimp with garlic powder and salt and pepper.

3. In a small bowl combine the paprika and flour.

4. Crack the eggs into another small bowl and whisk.

5. Place the panko crumbs in another small bowl.

6. Dip the shrimp one by one into the flour mixture and then into the eggs and then into the panko crumbs.

7. Fry the shrimp in batches until they turn golden brown in color. This should take approximately 5 minutes.

8. Line a plate with paper towels.

9. Remove the shrimp from the deep fryer with a slotted spoon and drain them on the plate.

10. Serve with a dip of your choice.

22: Deep Fried Oreos

Did you know that Oreos taste even better fried?

Preparation time: 20 minutes

Serves: 10 servings

Ingredients

- Vegetable oil
- 1 large egg
- 1 cup of milk
- 2 teaspoons of vegetable oil
- 1 cup of pancake mix

- 1 packet of Oreo cookies
- Whipped cream

Directions

1. Heat the oil in a deep fryer until it reaches 375 degrees C.

2. In a small bowl combine the milk, eggs, and 2 teaspoons of vegetable oil and whisk together thoroughly.

3. Add the pancake mix to the egg mix and whisk together thoroughly.

4. Dip one Oreo at a time into the batter.

5. Fry in small batches until golden brown in color. This should take approximately 2 minutes.

6. Line a plate with paper towels.

7. Remove the cookies from the deep fryer using a slotted spoon and drain on the plate.

8. Serve with the whipped cream.

23: Deep Fried Dill Pickles

Did you know that pickles taste even better fried?

Preparation time: 20 minutes

Serves: 6 servings

Ingredients

- 2 eggs
- 1 cup of buttermilk
- 1 tablespoon of Worcestershire sauce
- ½ a teaspoon of hot pepper sauce (vinegar based)
- ¾ teaspoons of cayenne pepper
- ¼ teaspoon of seasoning salt
- ¼ teaspoon of garlic powder
- 1 cup of oatmeal
- 2 ¼ cups of all-purpose flour
- 1 teaspoon of salt
- ¾ teaspoon of ground black pepper
- 1 jar of dill pickle slices
- 1 cup of vegetable oil
- Salt
- Black pepper

Directions

1. Heat the oil in a deep fryer until it reaches 375 degrees C.

1. Combine the garlic powder, seasoning salt, cayenne pepper, hot sauce and Worcestershire sauce in a large bowl and whisk together thoroughly.

2. In a large bowl combine 2 cups of flour, cornmeal, ¾ teaspoon of black pepper and salt.

3. Drain the pickles and dip them into the milk mixture and then into the flour mixture.

4. Fry until golden brown in color. This should take approximately 10 minutes.

5. Line a plate with paper towels.

6. Remove the pickles from the deep fryer using a slotted spoon and drain on the plate.

7. Season with salt and pepper and serve.

24: Deep Fried Moroccan Potatoes

Sweet tasting deep fried Moroccan potatoes.

Preparation time: 25 minutes

Serves: 4 to 6 servings

Ingredients

- 1kg of potatoes
- ¾ teaspoons of salt
- ½ a teaspoon of paprika
- 1/8 teaspoon of white pepper
- 1/8 teaspoon of black pepper
- ½ a teaspoon of dried thyme
- 1/8 teaspoon of garlic powder

- 2 tablespoons of melted butter
- 4 cups of vegetable oil

Directions

1. Heat the oil in a deep fryer until it reaches 375 degrees C.

2. Peel the potatoes and slice them into bite sized cubes.

3. Wash and then drain the potatoes.

4. In a small bowl combine the garlic powder, thyme, black pepper, white pepper, paprika and salt, stir to combine and set to one side.

5. Fry the potatoes until they become golden brown in color and tender. This should take approximately 15 minutes.

6. Line a plate with paper towels.

7. Remove the potatoes from the deep fryer with a slotted spoon and drain on a plate.

8. Transfer the potatoes into a large bowl, drizzle the butter over them and toss to coat.

9. Toss with the spice mixture and serve.

25: Deep Fried French Fries

Who needs McDonalds when you can make your own French fries at home?

Preparation time: 20 minutes

Serves: 6 servings

Ingredients

- 6 large russet potatoes cut into French fries
- Vegetable oil
- Salt
- Ketchup

Directions

1. Heat the oil in a deep fryer until it reaches 375 degrees C.

2. In a large bowl of water soak the potatoes for approximately 30 minutes.

3. Add the potatoes to the deep fryer and cook for until they become golden brown in color. This should take approximately 5 minutes.

4. Line a plate with paper towels.

5. Remove the potatoes with a slotted spoon and drain them on the plate.

6. Sprinkle with salt and serve with ketchup.

26: Deep Fried Sausage

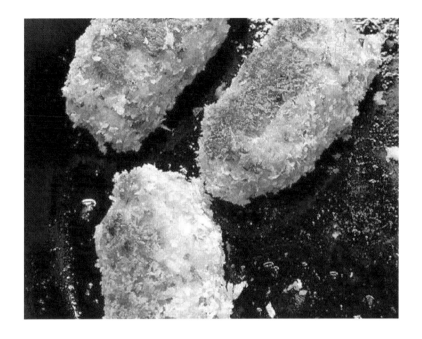

A simple sausage made irresistible in a deep fryer!

Preparation time: 45 minutes

Serves: 6 servings

Ingredients

- 1 pound of Italian sausage roll sliced into bite sized pieces
- 2 cups of Italian bread crumbs
- 1 cup of ground Parmesan cheese
- 3 large eggs, beaten
- Vegetable oil

Directions

1. Heat the oil in a deep fryer until it reaches 375 degrees C.

2. In a large bowl combine the Parmesan cheese and the bread crumbs.

3. In a separate large bowl, whisk the eggs.

4. Dip the sausages into the eggs and then into the bread crumb mixture.

5. Fry the sausages until they become golden brown in color. This should take approximately 5 minutes.

6. Serve with a side dish of your choice.

27: Deep Fried Cauliflower

If your kids hate cauliflower, fry them! They will be begging for seconds!

Preparation time: 16 minutes

Serves: 6 servings

Ingredients

- 1 large head of cauliflower cut into bite sized florets
- 2 large eggs, beaten
- 1 tablespoon of milk
- ¼ teaspoon of salt
- 1 ½ cups of flour
- 2 tablespoons of shredded parmesan cheese
- ¼ teaspoon of garlic powder
- ½ a teaspoon of dried thyme
- 1 teaspoon of dried oregano
- 1/8 teaspoon of paprika
- Cayenne pepper
- ¼ teaspoon of black pepper
- Vegetable oil

Directions

1. Heat the oil in a deep fryer until it reaches 375 degrees C.

2. In a large bowl combine the eggs, milk and salt and whisk together thoroughly.

3. In a large bowl combine the black pepper, cayenne, paprika, oregano, thyme, garlic powder, cheese and flour and stir together thoroughly.

4. Dip the florets into the egg mixture and then into the flour mixture.

5. Fry in batches until they become golden brown in color. This should take approximately 6 minutes.

6. Line a plate with paper towels.

7. Remove the cauliflower with a slotted spoon and drain on the plate.

8. Serve with a dip of your choice.

28: Deep Fried Plantain

A taste of the Caribbean, deep fried plantain is delicious!

Preparation time: 9 minutes

Serves: 2 servings

Ingredients

- 2 ripe plantains
- Vegetable oil
- Salt

Directions

1. Heat the oil in a deep fryer until it reaches 375 degrees C.

2. Peel and slice the plantain into round diagonal slices.

3. Fry the plantain until they turn golden brown in color. This should take approximately 5 minutes.

4. Line a plate with paper towels.

5. Remove the plantain from the deep fryer with a slotted spoon and allow them to drain on the plate.

6. Sprinkle with salt and serve.

29: Deep Fried Salmon

Cod isn't the only fish you can fry!

Preparation time: 30 minutes

Serves: 4 servings

Ingredients

- 4 salmon fillets, skinless
- 100 grams of plain flour
- 2 eggs, yolks separated

- 175 ml of ice water
- 2 tablespoons of vegetable oil
- Vegetable oil

Directions

1. Heat the oil in a deep fryer until it reaches 375 degrees C.

2. In a large bowl combine the 2 tablespoons of vegetable oil, the water, egg yolks and the flour.

3. In a separate small bowl whisk the egg whites until they make stiff peaks.

4. Add the egg white into the flour mixture and whisk until it becomes a smooth batter.

5. Dunk the salmon fillets into the batter and fry until they become golden brown in color, this should take approximately 10 minutes.

6. Line a plate with paper towels.

7. Remove the salmon fillets from the deep fryer and drain on the plate.

8. Serve with a side dish of your choice.

30: Deep Fried Ice-cream

I had to save the best until last! Bon appetite!

Preparation time: 10 minutes

Serves: 6 servings

Ingredients

- 750 ml of vanilla ice-cream
- 250 grams of digestive biscuits
- 2 large eggs
- 1 tablespoon of milk
- Sunflower oil
- 1cing sugar
- Maple syrup

Directions

1. Line a baking tray with parchment paper.

2. Use an ice-cream scoop to scoop out 6 servings onto the baking tray. (Do this quickly)

3. Place the baking tray into the freezer for 2 hours.

4. Transfer the biscuits into a large zip lock bag crush them with a rolling pin into fine crumbs.

5. Transfer the crushed biscuits into a shallow bowl.

6. Take the frozen ice-cream out of the freezer and roll them in the crushed biscuits. Put them back onto the baking tray and freeze them again for another 1 hour.

7. In a large bowl combine the milk and the eggs and whisk together thoroughly.

8. Remove the ice-cream from the freezer and dip them into the eggs and then into the crushed biscuits. Place the ice-cream back onto the baking tray and freeze for another 1 hour.

9. Heat the oil in a deep fryer until it reaches 375 degrees C.

10. Remove the ice-cream from the freezer and fry for 15 seconds.

11. Line a plate with paper towels.

12. Remove the ice-cream balls with a slotted spoon and drain on the plate.

13. Sprinkle with the icing sugar, drizzle with the maple syrup and serve.

Conclusion

Thank you for purchasing my book! I really hope you had just as much fun as I did making these recipes! There are so much more fried foods you can enjoy, unfortunately you only have 30 recipes here; however, I hope you have been inspired to search out some more fried food recipes so that you can continue enjoying hearty meals for many more days to come!

Author's Afterthoughts

Thanks ever so much to each of my cherished readers for investing the time to read this book!

I know you could have picked from many other books but you chose this one. So a big thanks for downloading this book and reading all the way to the end.

If you enjoyed this book or received value from it, I'd like to ask you for a favor. Please take a few minutes to post an honest and heartfelt review on Amazon.com. Your support does make a difference and helps to benefit other people.

Thanks!

Daniel Humphreys

About the Author

Daniel Humphreys

Many people will ask me if I am German or Norman, and my answer is that I am 100% unique! Joking aside, I owe my cooking influence mainly to my mother who was British! I can certainly make a mean Sheppard's pie, but when it comes to preparing Bratwurst sausages and drinking beer with friends, I am also all in!

I am taking you on this culinary journey with me and hope you can appreciate my diversified background. In my 15 years career as a chef, I never had a dish returned to me by one of clients, so that should say something about me!

Actually, I will take that back. My worst critic is my four years old son, who refuses to taste anything that is green color. That shall pass, I am sure.

My hope is to help my children discover the joy of cooking and sharing their creations with their loved ones, like I did all my life. When you develop a passion for cooking and my suspicious is that you have one as well, it usually sticks for life. The best advice I can give anyone as a professional chef is invest. Invest your time, your heart in each meal you are creating. Invest also a little money in good cooking hardware and quality ingredients. But most of all enjoy every meal you prepare with YOUR friends and family!

Printed in Poland
by Amazon Fulfillment
Poland Sp. z o.o., Wrocław